COUNTRIES OF THE SAHARA

COUNTRIES OF THE SAHARA

CHAD, MALI, MAURITANIA, NIGER, UPPER VOLTA, AND WESTERN SAHARA

BY HENRY GILFOND

FRANKLIN WATTS
New York | London | Toronto | Sydney | 1981
A FIRST BOOK

G
A GROLIER COMPANY

Cover design by Jackie Schuman

Photographs courtesy of:
Gerster/Rapho/Photo Researchers, Inc.: pp. 16, 51;
Gerster/Photo Researchers, Inc.: pp. 18, 54;
Englebert/Photo Researchers, Inc.: p. 35;
Alain Nogues/Sygma: p. 59;
Ray Witlin/United Nations: p. 26;
United Nations: p. 30;
UN/FAO World Food Program/F. Mattioli: p. 42.

Maps courtesy of Vantage Art, Inc.

Library of Congress Cataloging in Publication Data

Gilfond, Henry.
Countries of the Sahara.

(A First book)
Bibliography: p.
Includes index.
SUMMARY: Describes the history, geography, and way
of life of six arid African countries.
1.   Africa, West—Juvenile literature.
2.   Sahel—Juvenile literature. [1.   Africa, West.
2.   Sahel]   I.   Title.
DT471.G54   966   80-22697
ISBN 0-531-04271-5

CONTENTS

———1———
The Saharan Countries
I

———2———
The Many Peoples
7

———3———
Countless Languages
I I

———4———
The Potential for Plenty
I 3

———5———
Religion
20

———6———
Family
24

——— 7 ———
Education and Health
32

——— 8 ———
Chad
39

——— 9 ———
Mali
44

——— 10 ———
Mauritania
47

——— 11 ———
Niger
50

——— 12 ———
Upper Volta
53

——— 13 ———
Western Sahara
57

Bibliography
61

Index
62

To my friends in
Shinnecock Hills

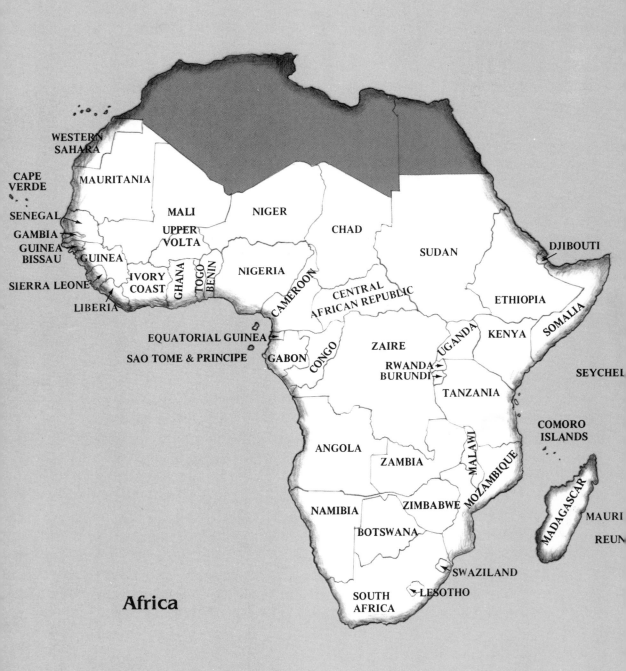

WESTERN
SAHARA

CAPE
VERDE

MAURITANIA

SENEGAL

GAMBIA
GUINEA
BISSAU

GUINEA

SIERRA LEONE

LIBERIA

MALI

UPPER
VOLTA

IVORY
COAST

GHANA

TOGO
BENIN

NIGER

CHAD

SUDAN

DJIBOUTI

NIGERIA

CAMEROON

CENTRAL
AFRICAN REPUBLIC

ETHIOPIA

SOMALIA

EQUATORIAL GUINEA

SAO TOME & PRINCIPE

GABON

CONGO

ZAIRE

UGANDA

RWANDA
BURUNDI

KENYA

SEYCHEL

TANZANIA

COMORO
ISLANDS

ANGOLA

ZAMBIA

MALAWI

MOZAMBIQUE

MADAGASCAR

MAURI

REUN

NAMIBIA

ZIMBABWE

BOTSWANA

SWAZILAND

SOUTH
AFRICA

LESOTHO

Africa

1
THE
SAHARAN COUNTRIES

Chad, Mali, Mauritania, Niger, Upper Volta, and even the disputed territory known as Western Sahara, were at one time part of, or the center of, powerful ancient African kingdoms and empires.

Chad, it is believed, was once the seat of an ancient and magnificent African culture. Mali was an essential element in the ancient empires of Mali and Songhai until those empires began to decline in the fifteenth century.

The Muslim Berbers, first, then the Muslim Arabs invaded and brought to an end the vast kingdom of Mauritania. Both Niger and Western Sahara, too, were parts of ancient and mighty African domains, until those domains were destroyed by conquering invasions.

European invaders entered the African arena between the fifteenth and eighteenth centuries. In a sudden surge of imperialism, England, France, Portugal, Holland, Germany, and even Spain and Italy, began to carve up the African continent into spheres of influence, protectorates, and colonies.

The dream of all these European countries was to build an empire. This struggle for empires would prove to be one of the causes, if not the main cause, for the outbreak of the First World War.

France was particularly spurred to action in Africa late in the nineteenth century, after its defeat by the Germans in the Franco-Prussian War of 1870. The French had been forced to cede Alsace-Lorraine, a huge and valuable piece of its territory, to the Germans. Their intention was to make up for that loss with the lands of Africa.

They chose to push into the Saharan regions of the continent and, in less than thirty years, the French tricolor flag flew over Chad, Mali, Mauritania, and Upper Volta. It took them only a little longer to add Niger to their empire.

Spain did not have the forces or the money with which to compete against the more powerful European countries. They managed to carve out for themselves, however, the extreme western area of the arid Sahara, two adjacent territories that were called, for a long time, Rio de Oro and Sekia el Hamra.

Before the French, even before the Berbers and the Arabs, Mali, Mauritania, and Chad had all been subject to numberless migrations, invasions, and wars. There had been wars between rival tribes, wars between kingdoms, wars between empires, and wars for liberation and independence. Nor is there too much peace in these lands today.

There has been and continues to be, in one measure or another, a constant struggle for power. There are deep-seated rivalries among the many tribes and ethnic groups in each of these countries. There are religious differences that make for riot and rebellion. There are coups and countercoups, revolutions that are sometimes very bloody. In Western Sahara, a guerrilla army is still fighting for the independence of their land, not from Spain, but from neighboring countries, Morocco and Mauritania.

Chad, Mali, Mauritania, Niger, Upper Volta, and the territory of Western Sahara are all very poor lands, among the poorest in the world. Yet, the conflict for control of these countries, as well as for freedom and equal rights, continues undiminished, and often violent.

THE LAND

The Sahara Desert is the dominant physical feature of all these countries. Only the Upper Volta is not touched by the desert, but it lies on the fringe of the Sahara, and the Sahara continues to claim more land with the years.

Upper Volta is in fact a vast plateau. It has a number of valleys that are formed by its rivers—the Black Volta, the White Volta, and the Red Volta—but the entire land, so close to the Sahara, is relatively dry and poor.

Only Mauritania and Western Sahara, of these countries, border on the Atlantic Ocean. Chad, Mali, Niger, and Upper Volta have no access to the sea. They are completely landlocked.

Chad does have a huge lake—Lake Chad, 9,946 square miles (25,760 sq km)—that spills over into Niger and Nigeria. Once, it is believed, Lake Chad was a great inland sea. Today, its maximum depth is no more than 23 feet (6.9 m). Its minimum depth is 5 feet (1.5 m). And geologists say that Lake Chad continues to dry up.

Southeast of the lake, Chad rises northward and eastward to mountain ranges on its borders with the Sahara and Sudan. The Tibesti range to the north rises to a height of 10,318 feet (3,145 m). The central part of the country is a savanna, that is, a flat, treeless grassland. In its south, there are the Shari River, marshlands, and the beginning of a tropical forest. But Chad is fully half desert.

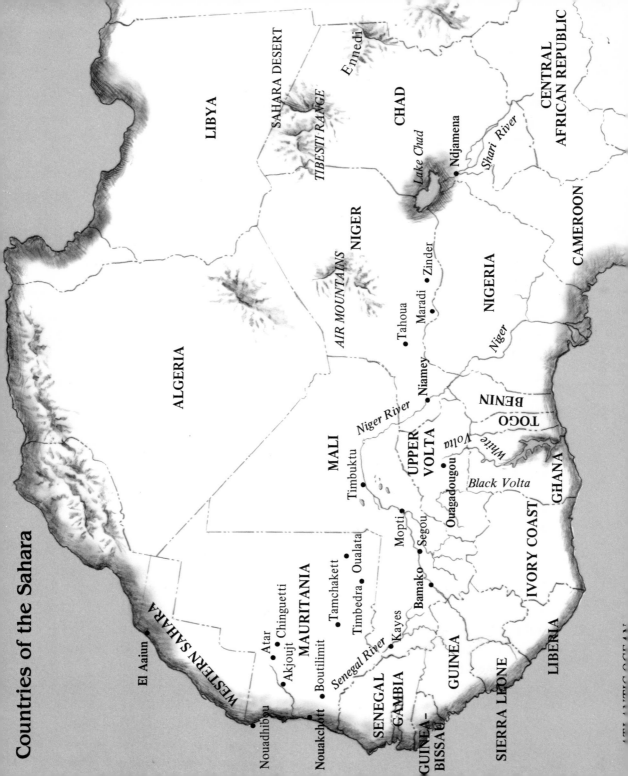

Countries of the Sahara

LIBYA

SAHARA DESERT

Ennedi

TIBESTI RANGE

CHAD

Lake Chad

Ndjamena

Shari River

CENTRAL
AFRICAN REPUBLIC

ALGERIA

NIGER

AIR MOUNTAINS

Tahoua

Maradi Zinder

NIGERIA

Niger

CAMEROON

WESTERN SAHARA

El Aaiun

Atar
Chinguetti
Akjoujt
Boutilimit
Nouadhibou
Nouakchott

MAURITANIA

Tamchakett

Timbedra Oualata

Senegal River

Kayes

MALI

Timbuktu

Mopti
Segou

Bamako

Niger River

Niamey

UPPER
VOLTA

Ouagadougou

White Volta

Black Volta

BENIN

TOGO

GHANA

IVORY COAST

SENEGAL

GAMBIA

GUINEA-
BISSAU

GUINEA

SIERRA LEONE

LIBERIA

The northern and central areas of Niger, too, are desert-land, broken only by the Air and Djado mountains, which rise to a height of 6,000 feet (1,800 m). Most of the country bordering the Sahara is a vast plateau, with a median height of 1,200 feet (360 m). The south of Niger is flat and treeless but, unlike the savanna of Chad, it can be cultivated to grow much needed crops because the Niger River flows through the region.

Mali is mainly flat and dry. It is utterly desolate in the north, but the central part of the country is watered by the Niger River, as well as the Baoulé, Bagoé, and Bakoy rivers. This area of the country has good pasture and soil in which to farm. Western Mali is savanna and scrubland. The entire flatness of the country is broken only by its dramatic sandstone mountains and plateaus.

Fully three-quarters of the land of Mauritania is desert, sandy and rocky Saharan territory broken only by an occasional oasis. The Senegal River waters about one-quarter of the country and allows for the growing of Mauritania's crops.

Western Sahara is almost entirely desert and arid. There is just about enough vegetation for the flocks of the nomads who wander far and wide to keep their animals alive.

VEGETATION

So much of this area in Africa is desert and so much of the rest of it flat, treeless grassland, with an almost constant need for rain, that vegetation is at best sparse.

There is millet and rice, some corn and cotton, vegetables, dates, and peanuts. But, except for peanuts, there is barely enough to keep the farmers and their families alive. When the scarce rain becomes even scarcer, in times of drought, then the people of this region have to face and endure starvation.

[5]

There are date palms on the oases that dot the desertlands. Where the land is watered by rivers or lakes, there is brushwood, acacia trees, soapberry trees, caper, swallowwort, baobab, and gonakie trees. There are even thin patches of woodland. But, while the greater part of this area lies within the torrid zone, there is little evidence of it in its vegetation. The arid Sahara is the dominant feature in these lands.

WILDLIFE

The wildlife in these countries is more like what we expect to find in Africa. There are lions and leopards, hyenas, jackals, cheetahs, elephants, hippopotamuses, rhinoceroses, giraffes, antelope —all the animals associated with the wildlife in tropical parts of the world. There are all the varieties of reptiles, including the deadly python and crocodiles. Some of the latter are considered sacred. The birds include ostriches, flamingos, pelicans, and the weaverbird, which feeds on the farmers' crops. Insects of every kind inhabit the land.

In the waters off Mauritania and Western Sahara there are dolphins and seals; and dorado, bonito, sea trout, and other fish. The dolphin is actually used by Mauritanian fishermen to help them in their fishing.

There is also a considerable number of freshwater fish in the rivers of the area, and particularly in Lake Chad.

It should be noted that hunting for trophies has cut down the wild animal population in this region, as elsewhere in the world. Some effort has been made to reduce the hunting and to preserve the wildlife, with, unfortunately, only minimal results.

2
THE MANY PEOPLES

As in most countries of Africa, there is an almost countless number of ethnic groups in Chad, Mali, Mauritania, Mali, Niger, and Western Sahara. Migrations of families through the years, often of whole clans, in search of good pasture for their flocks and good ground for growing their crops, undoubtedly helped create this conglomeration of different peoples in each of the African countries. Constant invasions, not only by Europeans but also by African tribes, chiefdoms, kingdoms, and even empires, must account, too, for much of this mixture of peoples throughout the continent.

The Hausa people constitute about 50 percent of the population of Niger. But there are Hausa in Chad as well. The Fulani people make up 15 percent of Niger's population. But there are Fulani in Upper Volta and Chad, as well.

Tuaregs are in Mali, Niger, and Western Sahara. Tuaregs are classified as a Caucasoid (white) people, with skin coloring varying from light to brown, and hair that varies from straight to wavy and curly. The Maure, who constitute 75 percent of the population of Mauritania, are classified as Caucasoid, too. Actually, they are more akin to the Moors than to any other group.

And the Voltaic people of Mali, 12 percent of Mali's population, are most likely related to the Mossi, another Voltaic people, of Upper Volta.

Of the other people in these countries, there are the Bobo and Mande of Upper Volta; and the Djermas, who constitute 23 percent of the peoples in Niger. In addition to its Tuaregs and Voltaic peoples, there are the Peruels and the Songhai in Mali, each with their own gods, their own customs, and their own way of life. The majority of the people in Mali, however, are Mandes. The Mandes themselves are split into a number of different ethnic groups, such as the Bambara, the Malinke, and the Sarakole.

There are some thirty-three ethnic groups in Chad. Some 30 percent of its people are Arabs, and 45 percent are the African Saras. In addition, there are the Maba, Dadjo, Tama, Massalat, Wadalan, Toubou, and many, many more.

The Fulbe, Toucoleur, Soninke, Wolof, and Bombara join with the Maure in Mauritania. In Western Sahara, among others, there are the Reguibat, the Delim, and the Izarguen.

Since all these countries except Western Sahara were French colonies, it is not surprising that a number of French people still reside there. There are about three thousand in Mali, two thousand in Mauritania, and about five thousand in both Chad and Niger.

It should be noted, too, that the French attitude to the peoples of their colonies was quite different from that of the other Europeans. They never separated themselves from the Africans. There were no separate washrooms, one for blacks, one for whites; no separate schools, churches, or park benches. This does not say that the French did not exploit their colonies, but certainly there was less overt discrimination against their colonial peoples than was seen with other European settlers.

Discrimination did seem to take hold in these countries, however, once they achieved their independence. Actually, there had always been some rivalry, even antagonism, among the different ethnic groups of these lands. The antagonism grew sharper as each group fought for the position of leadership in the governments of the new independent states.

This situation is especially acute in Mauritania, where the majority, light-skinned Maure people have attempted to dominate and suppress the black minorities. In addition, Mauritania has a full-blown caste system that hampers any attempt to unify its peoples. There are six different castes in Mauritania, ranging from the nobility to a virtual slave caste.

The *hassan,* or warrior caste, the fighting men of Mauritania, constitute the cream of the nobility. The *marabout,* or religious caste, is considered nobility too.

The third caste, in descending order, is the *zenaga.* The zenagas are the descendants of the Berbers (North Africans) who were conquered by the Arabs. Craftspeople, people who work with iron, wood, silver, copper, and leather, make up the fourth caste.

The *griots* come next. They are the poets and musicians. While the Muslim Maure have a great love for both poetry and music, they look down on the griots. They also fear them. Griots are supposed to possess great mystical powers.

The sixth and lowest caste in this Maure social system is made up of the so-called black Maures. These people had been, historically, the slaves of the nobility in Mauritania. When Mauritania was a French colony, the French decreed that slavery was illegal. Still, to this day, the so-called black Maure, now called freedmen, remain on the farms and in the households of their former masters, performing the same servile work they have done for countless years.

With so many different ethnic groups inhabiting each new African country, and the paralyzing caste systems that make up the social order as well, it is not difficult to understand the problems involved in creating a national unity for the health and well-being of their struggling communities.

3

COUNTLESS LANGUAGES

French, inherited from the days of colonialism, is the official language of Chad, Mali, Mauritania, Niger, and Upper Volta. Spanish might be the official language of Western Sahara, if Western Sahara were recognized as an independent country. But in all these countries there are as many languages and dialects of languages spoken as there are different ethnic groups.

There is a good deal of Arabic spoken, particularly in the Islamic sections of these countries. Both French and Arabic are official languages in Mauritania. While many of the African tongues are definitely related, the Fulani will no more understand Hausa people than the average American will understand the speech of Portugal.

In Mali, a variety of Mandingo and Sudanic languages and dialects are spoken, including Hausi, Songhai, Fulani, Tamashek, Djerma, and a host of other African tongues, as well as Arabic.

The people of Upper Volta speak Mossi, Samol, Lobi, and Gourounsi. In Chad, the Toubou people speak either Tedaga or Dazaga, depending on the area in which they live. Sara is spoken by the majority of the people, but others speak Kanembou, Ouddai, Massa, Gorane, and Bora Mandaba.

Wolof and Tukulor are the principal African tongues in Mauritania, but the vast majority of its people, the Maure, speak Arabic, or Hassaniyah, as it is called in Mauritania.

Languages can cause disharmony. The great number of languages in the African countries has hindered considerably the efforts of their leaders to bring about a unified national spirit among their peoples.

It should be noted that all the estimated eight hundred African languages are considered, by people who make a comparative study of languages, to be highly developed and expressive. They are languages that depend much on the tonal quality with which they are spoken. The meaning of a word will depend upon the manner in which it is pronounced.

The African "talking drums," used for sending messages over long distances, incidentally, duplicate almost perfectly the quality of African speech.

4
THE POTENTIAL FOR PLENTY

There is richness of untapped minerals in all the lands of Chad, Mali, Mauritania, Niger, Upper Volta, and even in the deserts of Western Sahara. For all the arid areas that cover much of these countries, there is grass enough to feed their herds of cattle, their flocks of sheep and goats. Except when rain is scarce, there is enough arable acreage to grow their crops. There is a wealth of precious ores to be mined in their hills. Mauritania and Western Sahara have an abundance of fish in the South Atlantic Ocean, and Chad has the freshwater fish of the huge Lake Chad.

Still, without exception, these countries are among the poorest in the world. When each of them achieved independence, there was a significant loss of technical personnel. The French had made little effort to train the Africans for technical jobs. When the European technicians left Africa, Africans had to begin almost from scratch to teach their peoples how to run the machines and repair them. And they had neither enough schools nor enough teachers for that essential purpose. The fault is being remedied now, but slowly, with assistance from the United States, the People's Republic of China, Yugoslavia, North Korea, the Soviet Union, the Federal Republic of Germany, and others.

Agriculture is the mainstay of these countries, with the exception of Western Sahara. Ninety percent and more of the people in these countries live in the rural areas, growing a variety of crops.

For the most part, the farms are small and the people grow just enough to keep themselves alive on millet and sorghum, two grains that form the staples of their diet. This is called subsistence farming. When there is a drought, as there was from 1968 till 1974, the peoples of these countries are faced with actual starvation. Fortunately, at that time they were supplied with food by the United States and other countries, as well as by international help organizations.

In addition to the millet and sorghum, Mali, Mauritania, Upper Volta, and Chad have considerable rice crops. Chad, where rice has grown wild for centuries in the flood zones of its rivers and along the lakeshores, invested heavily in a program to expand its rice yield. But to date, the investment has not paid off, neither in the production of rice nor the consuming of it.

Peanuts are grown in abundance in Niger, Mali, Upper Volta, and Chad. Peanuts are Chad's third or fourth largest crop. The exporting of peanuts brings Niger 50 percent of its revenues from abroad. Cotton, too, is grown, in sufficient quantities to export, by Niger, Mali, Upper Volta, and Chad.

Significant crops of sugarcane and corn are harvested in Mali and Upper Volta. Dates and gum arabic are grown and exported by Mauritania. Gum arabic is used as a thickener in the preparation of pills, as well as in the manufacturing of candy.

All these countries have made a considerable effort to bring in modern farming equipment and techniques, with some success. However, the great majority of farmers, either for lack of technical know-how or because of their traditions, still work their lands as their fathers did, and their fathers before them.

This holds true for the herders in these countries as well. Herding cattle, sheep, and goats is a major activity in Chad, Mali, Mauritania, Niger, and Upper Volta. It is the most productive activity in Western Sahara, where most of the people are nomadic herders.

In addition to the keeping of these animals, Niger receives about 20 percent of its revenues from other countries from its exports of meat, skins, and hides. A principal export of Chad is live cattle, as well as beef. Mali, Mauritania, and Upper Volta, too, export livestock and related products. Droughts cut into this production, but it still remains a major source of income for these countries.

There are several thousand professional fishermen fishing the waters of Lake Chad. Their annual catch amounts to 121,000 tons (100,000 m.t.) of fish. Mauritania gets an income of about three million dollars annually, exporting its fishing catch.

Someday mining may rescue all these African countries from poverty. Each has a considerable amount of unmined ores. Even Western Sahara has sizable deposits of phosphates and iron ore. Phosphates are used as fertilizers in modern agriculture.

Mali, Niger, and Mauritania have rich iron ore deposits as well, but only Mauritania mines enough iron ore to export it. The difficulty all these countries face in extracting the precious ores from the ground is their lack of power facilities, as well as woefully inadequate transportation facilities. They lack the railroads or the truck roads to transport the material.

Uranium is present in Niger, Upper Volta, and Chad. Mauritania exports some copper, which is also to be found in Upper Volta. There are deposits of manganese in Mali, Upper Volta, and Mauritania. There is bauxite in Upper Volta and Mali, limestone in Niger and Mali. Kaolin, used in ceramics and as a

Fishermen along the Bani River in Mali empty their traps.

filler for paper and textiles, is found in Mali, as is some gold.

Some gold, as well as precious marble, is also found in Upper Volta. Tin and tungsten may be mined in Chad, gypsum in Niger, sulphur in Mauritania. And the United States, France, and Italy have invested a great deal of money to investigate the possibility of discovering oil in Niger and Mauritania.

To date, the oil has still to be discovered. As for the ores, with minor exception, the reports do not indicate the great finds that would make mining profitable. And even if such finds were discovered, the enormous amount of capital needed to provide the adequate power and transportation facilities is close to prohibitive. Mining, as a major activity and revenue provider for these African countries, is still a long way off.

Industry in these countries is meager, despite governmental efforts to industrialize their peoples. Significant aid from foreign countries has not helped too much either.

For example, the People's Republic of China has built in Mali a textile factory, a tannery, a sugar mill, and a cigarette and match factory. Yugoslavia has built a cannery in Mali; North Korea, a ceramics factory; the Soviet Union, a cement plant; the Federal Republic of Germany, a peanut-oil mill; and the European Common Market, a modern slaughterhouse. Still, not more than 1 percent of the entire population of Mali is involved with industry and commerce.

The other countries have only a slightly better showing. About 5 percent of the peoples of Upper Volta are employed in industry, commerce, and service, combined. Chad may have as many as 4 percent of its people in industry and the crafts.

Chad has some processing plants for peanuts and rice, a dairy plant, flour mill, sugar refinery, textile mill, and brewery. All the plants and mills, however, operate on a small scale.

Mauritania has a flour mill, a sugar refinery, a match factory, and a cement works. The cement works is financed by the People's Republic of China.

It is obvious that industry is at a rather impoverished level in these countries, and that the investments of foreign capital have done very little to improve the situation.

At one time in the cultures of these people, handicraft attained the level of fine art. This was true of their stone and wood carvings, their pottery, the jewelry made of gold and silver, their decorating of gourds for drinking cups and containers, their basket weaving and leatherwork. Handicraft, as practiced today, does not quite reach the level of quality of the past; still, a great number of artisans in this region continue to employ their skills, making everything from hair ornaments to tribal ceremonial masks. They are also involved in making practical items such as sandals, pouches, clothing out of leather, gourds for storing grain, and wood statuettes for ritual purposes.

It should be noted that the Arab influence on the making of jewelry or other work in silver, gold, copper, and brass is marked by some excellent work with filigree; the use of fine metal wire.

However, while this handicraft does bring in some revenue at the marketplaces throughout the region, it brings in comparatively little. Certainly it does not significantly alter the economic poverty of these countries.

The Sahara, the largest desert in the world,
covers about one-third of the continent of Africa.
Still, it continues to drift southward,
claiming land where villages and towns once stood.

5

RELIGION

More than half the people of this area in Africa are Muslims. While only 20 percent of the population of Upper Volta follow the faith of Islam, 52 percent of the people in Chad, 65 percent of the people in Mali, 85 percent in Niger, and almost 100 percent in Mauritania are practicing Muslims.

Christians constitute 5 percent or less of the populations in Chad, Mali, Niger, and Upper Volta. The old, traditional African faiths are followed by the rest of the population in these countries and, in some measure, by those who profess to be Muslims.

Islam was brought to this area by Muslim traders and craftsmen, mostly from the northern regions of Africa. They had little difficulty converting the people of these lands to their faith, but the Africans took what they wanted to believe from Islam and disregarded completely or deemphasized the rest.

The Africans liked Islam's promise of eternal life and its tolerance of their own traditional beliefs. It was easy enough for them to put on the Muslim white flowing robe and to pray in public. It was simple enough for them to take on Muslim names and to accept Allah as the all-powerful God. Allah was just another name for their own traditional all-powerful god.

But, they still maintain their beliefs in spirits and magic. Their ancestors and traditional spirits are still to be consulted and appeased in all matters relating to the family, their health, and the harvesting of their crops.

They carry verses of the Koran, Islam's holy book, copied on pieces of paper. They carry them, however, not as indications of their piety, but as traditional charms, charms supposed to possess magic powers.

There are "five pillars of faith" in Islam:

1. All Muslims must say, at least once in their lifetime, "There is no God but Allah, and Muhammad is his prophet."

2. Muslims must pray five times a day: at dawn, at noon, in the midafternoon, at sunset, and after nightfall.

3. Muslims must be charitable, especially to the needy.

4. Muslims must fast during Ramadan, the ninth month in the Muslim calendar, the month in which Allah sent down the Koran. The fast lasts, each day, from sunup to sundown. Only nursing mothers, soldiers on the march, and the sick are exempt. According to Muslim belief, the gates of paradise are open during Ramadan, the gates of hell shut, and the devil in chains.

5. If possible, once in his or her lifetime, the Muslim should make a pilgrimage (*hajj*) to Mecca.

Most of these pillars are easy enough for the Africans to observe. Very few, of course, can make the *hajj* to Mecca, in Saudi Arabia, but they will make journeys to the graves of men whom they consider saintly.

It is interesting to note, too, that while so many men have

[21]

adopted the faith of Islam, the number of Muslim women in these countries is considerably smaller. The women seem to prefer to hold on to the old African faiths.

Traditional African faiths, though there are a variety of names for the gods and spirits, have much in common. They all have a supreme and almighty god, but this god is too far away from them to be reached by prayer or sacrifice. There are, however, any number of lesser gods that control the fates of people on earth. The nature of these gods will depend on the area in which a people live. A rain god, by whatever name, will be common to those who inhabit the dry Saharan region. There will be river gods for those who depend on rising waters in their rivers for their crops. There are gods of thunder and of lightning, all nature gods. These can be prayed to, and sacrifices may be made to them to ensure good hunting, good fishing, good crops.

In addition, there are innumerable spirits, including the spirits of ancestors. These, according to the traditional beliefs, constantly interfere in the social and economic life of the people, in everything from family affairs to the well-being of an entire village.

They can do good or evil. They control the weather, the nature of the harvest, the supply of fish, and the outcome of a hunting expedition. They can punish or reward. They can make people ill, or even kill them. They can also cure wounds and sickness.

All agree that the spirits demand set rituals and sacrifice, if they are to be reached by the ordinary people. To reach them, to discover what is causing an illness in the family, some bad luck with the crops, or any other misfortune, a man will go to a diviner, the most religious person in his community.

The diviner will read the throw of bones or stones, or the entrails of a chicken, to divine the cause of his client's complaint. Then he will prescribe a cure. The cure may be no more than a talisman, an amulet, or some kind of charm. Most likely it will require, in addition, some sacrifice to get the spirit to temper its ill will and to remove its curse from the afflicted client.

The sacrifice generally depends on the affluence of the client. If he can afford it, he will be asked to sacrifice a goat. More often, he will sacrifice a chicken.

After the sacrifice, the slaughtered chicken or goat is cooked and all the participants in the ritual enjoy a hearty meal.

6

FAMILY

The family is the most important social and economic unit in Africa, as it is almost everywhere else in the world. Modern influences and pressures have tended to break up this unit in a number of highly industrialized cities, particularly in America and Europe, but they have scarcely touched the continent of Africa.

The father is still the undisputed head of the family. He may consult with his wife before making a family decision, as is the custom with some African peoples, but it is he who makes the decision.

He is the worker of the family, though his wife, or wives, and children do their share of labor in sowing the crops, weeding, harvesting, and taking care of whatever animals they possess. Polygamy is permissible; that is, a man may have more than one wife. Generally, however, he can't afford more than one. The Africans still pay for their brides. But, if a man has more than one, Islamic law demands that he treat his wives equally, giving each one the same care and attention.

The number of wives a man has goes a long way toward

determining his status in his village or camp. In fact, a relatively rich man is expected to have more than one wife.

Wealthy villagers generally live in a house with a galvanized iron roof. They will also have modern latrines. They will sometimes have cement floors.

Except in the urban centers, the people build their homes of whatever material they can lay their hands on. The traditional house is made of adobe brick or layer on layer of soft mud; the first layer of mud is allowed to dry before the next layer of mud is applied.

These houses generally have straw roofs shaped like cones. Their floors are dirt or clay. They have a low front door that is closed by a mat.

The nomads live in tents, usually set up in rows, as they move from place to place. The job of setting up the tents is generally left to the women, who complete their task in just about two hours. All but one of the tents is to house the clan of families. One tent is for housing the nomads' animals during the night. Sometimes a thorn enclosure is built around the entire encampment for protection against intruders, both animal and human.

Often, too, these nomads will dig wells in the dry land to get the water they need for both their animals and themselves.

In the larger urban centers, the families live in adobe houses. The houses are set flush with the streets. Generally there are no windows facing the street, but there is an opening from the house into an interior court. They are built this way because, after the Islamic tradition, the women of the family must be kept out of view.

A rural woman sweeps the floor of her open-air kitchen in a village in Upper Volta.

All sleep on straw mats or beds made of twigs.

Outside these urban centers, the landscape has its share of shantytowns. These are small settlements of people who cannot afford the city houses and live in anything they can erect to keep them from the streets.

There is a general shortage of housing in the cities and larger towns, and this, along with the lack of jobs in the cities, has sent many adventurous young Africans back to the villages and farms, and back to the bosom of their families.

WOMEN

Women, according to Islamic law, are second-class citizens. Though respected more by non-Islamic peoples of this region, they're still treated, for the most part, as inferior to men. Their principal duties are to tend to the house, work the farm, and bear children. Nothing is more important to the African male than the continuation of his name and family, if only so that he, too, may be worshiped as an ancestor.

Still, especially in the urban centers, women have made advances toward equal treatment. They are beginning to be heard in political councils, as well as in the marketplace and, to a lesser degree, in industry. There is, for example, a National Women's Movement in Islamic Mauritania, and several women have been elected to seats in the National Assembly, the governing body of the country.

Women, however, are still bought into arranged marriages. There has been some opposition to this practice, again particularly in urban centers. Young people want to choose their own wives or husbands. They are opposed to the idea of purchase, as something resembling the buying of slaves. But, tradition dies slowly, and the opposition to tradition has not moved too quickly or too far.

CHILDREN

Children remain the most important element in the African family. It is the children who carry forward the family name and tradition.

They are introduced to the traditions of their people early. They are taught how to survive in the environment in which they live; how to avoid dangerous animals, insects, snakes; how to find shelter from the elements of nature; how to find the food to keep themselves alive.

They are taught how to suffer privation, the hunger that comes with the frequent droughts in the region. They are also taught early how to take on family chores, like tending to the family crop, or the family herd of animals. As the children grow older, they are expected to go through certain set rituals that will transform them from children into men and women.

The rituals for the girls are simple. No great importance is attached to them. Girls are expected to be educated for marriage. When the boys are just about ready for the rites marking their passage into adulthood, the girls are housed, kept apart from any male contact, ready to be married off.

The rites for the boys are not only strenuous, they are painful and secret. No woman or outsider may witness them. They are the rites of initiation, of death and rebirth. The Sara people call it *yo-ndo*. Other peoples have other names for similar rituals.

The ritual of death and rebirth goes back to prehistoric times and has pervaded almost every civilization we know, from the Greek to the present.

The *yo-ndo* takes place at a traditional site under the direction of *nge-kor-bang-ndo* (the one who opens the road to the camp). Hundreds of boys, each accompanied by a guardian, may travel hundreds of miles away from their village to this camp. They may make this journey, at different time intervals, for as many as five to ten years or more, each time moving further into their initiation into manhood.

We do not know very much about these initiation rites because they are secret. But we do know that they are painful, sometimes humiliating. We know, too, that in addition to all the ordeals, the boys must make public confessions of whatever sins they think they may have committed. They must also learn by heart all the traditions and customs of their people. Finally, they all learn a secret language, a language spoken only by the initiates.

Curiously, a conglomeration of boys participate in these rituals, boys coming from different clans and tribes and speaking different languages. When they are through with their rites, they still will not be able to speak each other's language, but they will have the secret language in common. It is the common language that creates a bond of friendship, relationship, and loyalty among them for the rest of their lives.

DIET

The family diet depends on where the family lives. The nomads eat the meat of goats and sheep, milk, and dates. When they can,

they trade these staples for grains and vegetables. The farmers' families, for the most part, live on millet and vegetables. Sometimes, if they are near water, they can add some fish to their diet. In other areas, cassava, sweet potatoes, and other roots are available.

On the whole, the diets are poor in both proteins and carbohydrates. There is little resembling a balanced diet in these countries. When there is a drought, such as the droughts from 1968 to 1974, the size of the crops shrinks and there is not enough grass on which to pasture the nomads' animals. It is at such times that the whole area suffers a killing starvation.

Even in the nomadic families of Niger, children help with the chores. This young girl watches as livestock come to drink the water she has taken from a well and poured into hollow logs for them.

7
EDUCATION AND HEALTH

The African people have always been concerned with the education of their children. For the parents, from the beginning, it was most important to teach their children how to survive. Home was school for the African children. There were no other schools. For a good many African children, there still is no other school but home.

When the Muslims invaded Africa, they brought with them their *marabout*s (religious teachers) to aid in the conversion of the African people from their traditional religions to Islam. The *marabout*s set up the first formal schools in this part of the continent. But the aims of their education were quite limited. They did not teach the children how to read or write. They taught no arithmetic. The purpose of the *marabouts* was to instill in the minds of children the religious laws of Islam. To that end, the children spent countless hours memorizing texts from the Koran, Islam's holy book. They did not read or write down the text, they just repeated it, after the *marabout*, until they knew it by heart.

Western-style education—reading, writing, and arithmetic —was not introduced into this part of Africa until after the end of World War I, in the 1920s.

[32]

Protestant and Catholic missionaries set up their small schools, primarily to bring Christianity to the African people. However, they also taught the primary subjects to their pupils, both in French and Arabic. Later, the French colonial government contributed funds to these schools and erected some of their own. The process of educating this entire area, however, was very slow, mainly because there never was enough money put into the effort.

With independence, there has been a considerable increase in educational activity in this part of the African continent. There has been a general recognition, particularly among government leaders, that the educational level of their peoples has to be dramatically improved. They know that education is essential for a strong and healthy nation, for a nation that is unified in its purpose and its goals. They know that education is necessary to the development of their natural resources, their agriculture, and industry. They know that education is imperative to lift their countries out of the dire poverty they inherited with their freedom.

But education costs money, and there is very little money in the treasuries of these lands. Each of these countries established a ministry of education. Elementary schools were built, along with a scattering of secondary, vocational, and agricultural schools. They even built mobile schools to reach the children of the wandering nomadic people. But the number of schools is still woefully small; books and other schoolroom equipment are severely lacking; and a minimal number of their teachers are adequately prepared to teach.

In the 1960s, most of these African governments decreed compulsory primary education. All of them made primary education free. But today only 15 percent of the children of Mali attend school, and only 8 percent in Niger and 7 percent in Upper Volta. Less than 20 percent of the children of Chad, which has the best attendance, go to school.

School attendance, despite these sad numbers, has been on the increase in recent years, but there are many reasons why the governments in this area of Africa have not been able to come close to realizing their goal of universal education for their peoples.

First, there is the suspicion, by the Muslim population, of anything but the teachings of Islam. Muslims don't like sending their children to public schools.

Second, it has been almost impossible to set up anything like permanent schools for the children of the wandering nomads.

Third, much as so many peoples respect, admire, and want education for their children, they fear the effect of school learning on their local and tribal traditions and customs.

Fourth, parents claim that they need the children to help at home, with the farming, with the tending to their flocks, and with household chores. In many areas, the parents actually won't allow their children to attend school.

Fifth, though the enrollment of girls and women in the schools is constantly, if slowly, increasing, religious and traditional customs would have the girls at home, getting themselves ready for marriage.

Sixth, and very basically, the governments in this African region just don't have the funds to neutralize the fear of education among their peoples. They certainly don't have the money to provide their peoples with an educational system adequate to their needs.

Although the literacy level in most countries of the Sahara is very low, efforts are being made to improve the educational systems. Here, children in Niger participate in an experimental television teaching program.

Literacy in this part of Africa has inched up in recent years. But the overwhelming majority still can neither read nor write French, Arabic, or any other language.

Chad, with the highest literacy in the area, has a literacy rate of only 7 percent. Upper Volta has a literacy rate that has been estimated at anywhere from 5 to 7 percent. Niger, Mali, and Mauritania have a literacy rate of 6 percent, or less.

Some effort has been made in these countries to educate their peoples by means of radio and television programs. But Upper Volta has one television set for every thousand people in the country. The other countries don't even reach that level of affluence. Mauritania has 64 radios for every 1,000 of its people; and that is high, compared to Niger's 36, Chad's and Upper Volta's 16, and Mali's 14.

The educational problems in this part of Africa would seem to be insurmountable. They are not. But as long as these countries remain so terribly poor, the education of these people will remain lower than most other people in the world.

HEALTH

Health is a major problem in this area of Africa. Malaria, sleeping sickness, blinding eye infections, tropical ulcers, pneumonia, amebic dysentery, and tuberculosis are rampant. Cholera has finally been checked. There has been no cholera in Africa since 1977. Leprosy is being contained, but is still widespread. And there is such a shortage of medical personnel and medicines that visitors are advised to bring their own medication with them.

Life expectancy in these countries is no more than 41 years. Life expectancy for men in the United States is 68.7 years, for women 76.5 years.

In the United States we consider our infant mortality, 14 deaths per 1,000, high. In Upper Volta there are 182 infant deaths for every 1,000 born. There are 120 in Mali, 160 in Chad, 200 in Niger, and 187 in Mauritania.

Poor sanitation and polluted waters contribute much to these diseases, the infant mortality, and the short lifespan of these peoples. Poor health facilities, the lack of doctors, nurses, and hospital beds, do not help the situation.

There may be 150 doctors for all of Mali's six million people; that's one doctor for 40,000 possible patients. Upper Volta, Niger, Chad have fewer doctors. By recent count of the World Health Organization (of the United Nations), Mauritania did not have 75 doctors ready to practice medicine.

There just are not enough hospitals, not enough clinics, not enough nurses and technical assistants, and certainly not enough medical personnel to take care of the enormous health problems in these countries. The few doctors there are, live in the more thickly populated areas; people who live in the more arid and less populated regions must travel miles to get any kind of medical aid.

This lack of doctors has done nothing to lessen the reliance of so many of the peoples of these countries on their traditional methods of diagnosing their illnesses and trying to cure them. Many still believe their sicknesses are caused by evil spirits, witchcraft, and black magic. So many still visit their "medicine men" to discover the reasons for their ailments, by way of some magical process like reading entrails or casting stones. Then, to cast off the evil, they will wear amulets and charms, or make sacrifices of chickens.

Like other nations in other parts of Africa, these countries have concentrated on the prevention of disease, rather than on curing disease. This is almost a necessary procedure, since all medical facilities are so limited.

First, it has been recognized that the poor diets of the people contribute much to their illness. Consequently, the governments have begun to distribute milk and vitamins to their needy. Second, they have developed programs to teach their people the necessity for proper hygiene, through films, lectures, and books. The people are also taught the need for clean water, and for proper sanitary arrangements, including the development of good sewage systems to carry away polluting human and animal wastes. They are also being taught to fight rodents and insects that infest their homes. Finally, the government sends around teams of medics and paramedics to examine the ailing, particularly the children, and to inoculate them with disease-fighting serums.

The fight for health, it is obvious, is largely a battle in which education is a most important weapon. As with any other educational program, however, money is a very essential ingredient. According to estimates by the World Bank, $3 to $4 billion a year could take care of polluted waters all over the world within ten years. Polluted water is largely responsible for the illnesses of Africa. Although $30 billion is quite beyond the reach of these African countries, it is not beyond the reach of a world that would be rid of these African diseases.

It might be noted that the annual death rate in the United States is 9 per 1,000. In Chad, Mali, Mauritania, Niger, and Upper Volta an average of more than 24 of every 1,000 die every single year.

8
CHAD

The Republic of Chad, its official name, is almost as large as California, Arizona, New Mexico, and Nevada combined— 495,755 square miles (1,284,000 sq km). But half the country is covered by nothing but the sands of the Sahara Desert. It has a population of less than 4.5 million people.

Some 95 percent of its inhabitants live in the rural areas, mostly in the southern regions of the country, where they can eke out a living growing just enough crops to keep their families alive. The population thins out as the country moves north approaching the Sahara. The land grows dry, the crops become sparse, and the nomads move their flocks from place to place, looking for whatever pasture is available.

The largest city and capital of Chad, Ndjamena, called Fort Lamy when Chad was a French colony, has a population of about 224,000. There are some seven or eight other urban centers in Chad with no more than 10,000 to 50,000 in population. In the northern region of the country there are just a few towns with no more than a few hundred inhabitants in each.

Yet, at one time, Chad was a rich and perhaps one of the most flourishing areas in Africa. This was many thousands of years ago, before the sands of the Sahara covered so much of the land and when the entire region was much wetter than it is today.

Rock engravings that go back as far as 7,000 years ago have been found in the Tibesti and Borkou regions in the north of Chad. This is the work of artists who lived 5,000 years before the birth of Christ and gives evidence of an advanced civilization. The earliest engravings depict hunting scenes. Later engravings depict hunting and herding scenes. In the Ennedi area, there are rock paintings that go back as far as 3,000 years before Christ. Later rock paintings in this region depict the houses in which the people lived, and such labors as grain pounding and spinning.

The archeological work in the southern areas of Chad has not been as extensive, but there is evidence that the Lake Chad area has been inhabited since 500 B.C.

We have learned, too, from archeologists and anthropologists that Lake Chad was subject to a number of migrations of people from the north and east. The migrations brought any number of different ethnic groups to the area, but they are all generally referred to as the Sao people. According to legend the Sao were giants of superhuman strength and endurance. We do know that they lived in compact settlements and built walled cities of brick.

Most of what is known of the early history of Chad comes to us by way of oral tradition, stories told of ancient kings and ancient conquests. There were the Zaghawa kings, who claimed to come from Yemen and Ethiopia. There were the Muslim conquerors in the eleventh and twelfth centuries. For centuries Chad was a battleground for invaders, adventurers, and slave traders.

The last of these adventurers and slave traders was Rabah Zubayr, a Sudanese ex-slave. He had conquered the Bornu kingdom, now Nigeria, and threatened to overthrow the kingdoms of Chad. Chad called on France for help and the French sent their armies across the Sahara from Algeria to defeat the Sudanese troops of Zubayr, and to kill the invader.

This all happened in 1898. In 1900, France was in control of the entire region and declared it the Military Territory of Chad, under French domination.

In 1906, the French made a single territory of Chad and Ubangi-Shari (now the Central African Republic). In 1910, Chad became part of French Equatorial Africa, along with Gabon and Congo.

In 1940, after the fall of France to the Germans in World War II, Chad was the first African territory to rally to the Free French. They marched from Lake Chad, across the desert, to join the British fighting against the Germans in Africa.

In 1959, Chad became an autonomous member of the French community. On August 11, 1960, it became the independent Republic of Chad.

Francois Tombalbaye was Chad's first president. He was to be president of a country in almost constant tumult for fifteen years. At the bottom of the difficulties the country faced was the struggle for power beween the Muslims of the north and the peoples of the south.

Tombalbaye, who later changed his first name from Francois to Ngarta, outlawed opposition parties and created a one-party rule in 1962. In 1963, he imprisoned a number of officials and former ministers of the government, charging them with plotting his assassination.

Young villagers from a town near Lake Chad carry bowls of sand on top of their heads. With the sand, they will help make a dam to contain the waters of the lake.

In 1969, Tombalbaye was forced to call for help from the French to put down a growing Muslim rebellion.

A severe drought that lasted from 1968 to 1974 didn't help Tombalbaye. Thousands of people and tens of thousands of heads of cattle were killed by the drought. Tombalbaye made things worse by rejecting for political reasons the grain that the United States wanted to ship to the country to ease its famine.

In 1973, Tombalbaye arrested the commander of Chad's armies, General Felix Malloum, charging him with plotting a coup. Two years later, on April 3, 1975, Malloum's successor, Colonel Namari Djimet, was arrested on a similar charge. Eleven days later, on April 14, Tombalbaye was killed in a military coup and Malloum became president of a military junta that assumed supreme power in the country.

Chad's troubles were not over. Libya began to finance a rebel movement within Chad, the Chad Liberation Front (Frolinat). There were attempts to assassinate Malloum, and the fighting was incessant.

In March 1979, there was a cease-fire. Malloum was sent into exile in Nigeria, and Goukouni Oueddei, a Frolinat leader, became president of the country.

The cease-fire, however, was quickly broken. The rivalry for power between President Oueddei and his Prime Minister, Hissen Habrei, returned the country to civil war. Hundreds of people have been killed in the fighting, and peace seems to be a long way off for Chad.

9
MALI

The Republic of Mali, as it is known officially, covers an area of 464,873 square miles (1,204,021 sq km). It has an estimated population of 6.3 million. Mali is about the size of Texas and California combined.

Its capital and largest city is Bamako, with about 400,000 people. Mopti, Kayes, and Segou, its other large towns, are considerably smaller. Timbuktu, which was one of the greatest African trade centers in the fifteenth century, is no more than a legend today, with a population of less than 10,000. Ninety percent of Mali's people live in small towns and villages, farming, fishing, herding, and pursuing some kind of handicraft work.

Mali is scarcely less troubled, politically and economically, than Chad. But it has a history that surpasses Chad's for its glory.

Mali was a major part of the great African empires that flourished from the eighth through the sixteenth centuries: Ghana, Malinke, and Songhai. The Malinke kingdom of Mali, after which the present republic was named, was at the height of its powers about A.D. 1325, when it conquered Gao and Timbuktu.

The empires fell apart with the invasions of the Muslims, and, until the French came, the region was ruled by a number of local chieftains.

The French penetrated Soudan (now Mali) toward the end of the nineteenth century, but they met with considerable resistance on the part of Tukulor and Mandingo warriors. It was not until 1898, after seven years of war, that the French defeated the forces of the Malinke chief Samory Touré and established control of the region.

France was slow in giving Mali its independence.

In 1946, Soudan (Mali) was permitted to elect representatives to the French National Assembly. In 1958, Soudan became a member state of the French Community and was granted complete internal autonomy. In January 1959, Soudan and Senegal were joined to create the Mali Federation, but Senegal seceded from the union on August 20, 1960.

The next month, on September 22, 1960, Soudan withdrew from the French Community and declared itself the Republic of Mali.

Modibo Keita was its first president.

Keita established close relationships with the People's Republic of China and the Soviet Union. These actions were the cause of much unrest in the country, particularly in the army, which was pro-French. In 1967, Keita, to stem the tide against his political policies, dissolved Mali's national assembly and began to rule as a dictator.

Within a year, in 1968, the army executed a bloodless coup. Keita was out and Mali had a new president, Moussa Traoré. Mali is called a republic, but since 1968, it has been ruled by its army.

From 1946 through 1978, the United States has allocated about $100 million to Mali for economic aid. The principal interest of our country, with respect to Mali, is to help that country become self-sufficient in the production of the food it needs, to help it develop its livestock industry, and to help it remain free from the influence of foreign powers.

Between 1973 and 1975, the United States sent Mali 122,100 tons of emergency food, as well as $5 million in non-food assistance, during that country's severe drought.

The Peace Corps program of the United States, begun in 1961, has forty volunteers, as of this date, working in various agricultural activities with the people of Mali.

10
MAURITANIA

The Islamic Republic of Mauritania, its official name, is some 400,000 square miles (over 1,000,000 sq km) in area. Its area is not exact because, along with Morocco, Mauritania has laid claim to a huge part of what was once called Spanish Sahara, now, by some, Western Sahara.

Three-quarters of the country is desert and scrubland. A strip of land in the southern part of Mauritania, bordering the Senegal River, is fertile soil and provides the country with its essential foodstuff. It is Mauritania's desert, however, with its vast stores of iron ore and copper deposits, which is the country's source of wealth.

Mauritania, which is about three times the size of Arizona, has a population of only 1.5 million, which is just about the population of Denver, Colorado. Its largest city, and capital, Nouakchott, has a population of just about 135,000, which is about half the population of Erie, Pennsylvania. The other important cities of Mauritania, Nouadhibou, Atar, Chinguetti, Boutilimit, and Akjoujt, are considerably smaller.

Nouakchott, which was founded just about twenty years ago, is a little city with wide streets, a commercial district, public buildings, and residential areas. Still, a fringe of tents, inhabited by nomads, rings the city, reminding one that Mauritania is desert country.

Nouadhibou is the terminal of the only railroad in Mauritania. It is the country's main mineral port and a center of its fish canning and drying industry.

Atar was the capital of the conquering Almoravid kingdom of ancient times. The rock engravings of even more ancient times give evidence of perhaps prehistoric cultures in the area.

Chinguetti dates back to the fifteenth century and is considered the seventh holy city of Islam. Boutilimit houses the only advanced institute for the study of Islam in all West Africa.

Akjoujt, a newly constructed copper-mining town, is another spot in Mauritania which is rich in potential archeological finds of ancient cultures.

There are other small towns with much historical significance. Tamchakett was the old capital of Sanhadja, the Berber Confederation. Timbedra was the site of the capital of ancient Ghana. Oualata is a caravan city rich in historic architecture. Excavations are continually in progress in these areas, digging up interesting facts and artifacts of the great cultures of the past.

Mauritania looks on itself as a link between Arab Africa and black Africa. Its history makes this rather obvious.

Originally, Mauritania was inhabited by the black peoples of Africa. Slowly, they were forced back by invasions of Berbers from the north, sometime in the third and fourth centuries A.D.

By the eleventh century, the Almoravids, Berber Muslims, controlled not only northwest Africa, but also southern Spain and much of the disintegrating empire of Ghana. The Almoravid kingdom, however, began to fail, too, and the Berbers were conquered by Arab invaders, led by the conquering Beni Hassan tribes.

The Portuguese, Dutch, English, and French began to trade with the Mauritanians as early as the fifteenth century, but it was the French, beginning in the nineteenth century, who began to take control of the country. In 1904, France made a French protectorate of Mauritania. In 1920, Mauritania became a French colony.

It wasn't until 1960 that Mauritania became an independent nation, with Mokta Ould Daddah as its first president, and a fifty-man assembly.

The democratic nature of the republic, however, was limited. In 1964, a one-party system was established, and the powers of the assembly severely limited. The one progressive act of the president was to appoint a woman, Aissata Kane, to his cabinet, as minister of family welfare and social affairs.

The drought that hit all the countries of this region, however, unsettled Mokta Ould Daddah's reign. Eighty percent of the country's livestock, it was estimated, was destroyed by the drought. In 1978, an army coup, led by Lieutenant Colonel Moustapha Saleck, ousted Daddah. For almost a year, the country was governed by a thirteen-man Committee for National Recovery, headed by the Lieutenant Colonel.

An air crash which killed a number of high military officials forced the resignation of Saleck. The president of Mauritania currently is another army man, Lieutenant Colonel Mohamed Mahmoud Ould Louly.

11
NIGER

The Republic of Niger has an area of 490,000 square miles (1,267,000 sq km). It is larger than Texas and California combined but has a population of only about five million. Four-fifths of the country is arid desert. The rest is savanna, land that is suitable principally for herding cattle, sheep, and goats, and a limited amount of farming.

Its capital and largest city is Niamey, with a population of 130,000. This number increases and decreases, depending on the season of the year. During the dry season the nomads flock into the city. During the wet season, they leave it for whatever pastureland they can find.

Other cities in Niger are Zinder, Maradi, and Tahoua, none with a population over 20,000. Actually, they are no larger than moderately sized towns.

There is much evidence that in prehistoric times, long before the Sahara became a desert, this area of Africa was inhabited by prehistoric people. Archeologists believe that humans lived in this region as long as 600,000 years ago. It was most likely known by the Egyptians long before the beginnings of recorded history.

A bridge crossing the Niger River in Niamey, the capital of Niger.

Throughout history, Niger has been a battleground for numerous peoples, tribes, chiefdoms, and kingdoms. The empires of Ghana, Mali, Songhai, and Bornu fought for it. The Hausa states, the Djermas, the Fulani, and the Tuaregs fought for it. The Berbers and the Arabs fought for it as well. Finally, it was the French, in search of an empire, who came to Niger, to conquer it.

It did not come easily to the French. From 1901 till 1922, French armies fought against the stiff resistance of the Tuareg people, before they could call Niger, with comparative safety, a French colony.

Tribal loyalties are still very strong in Niger, making it very difficult to unify all its people into a single nation with a single national purpose.

In 1960, Niger became an independent republic, with Hamani Diori as its first president. Diori, like so many other African leaders, banned all political parties but his own. He was reelected president in 1965 and again in 1970.

Diori, again like other African leaders, fell victim to the drought which hit Africa, destroying whatever little economy Niger had. On April 15, 1974, Lieutenant Colonel Senyi Kountche, head of Niger's 2,500-man army, ousted Diori from his office. A twelve-man military government, with Kountche at the top, took over the reins of the country.

With Kountche as president, Niger has been ruled by a largely civilian government.

12

UPPER VOLTA

The Republic of Upper Volta is about the size of Colorado, with an area of 105,870 square miles (274,200 sq km). It has a population of about 6.5 million, not quite the population of Los Angeles, California.

About half the people of Upper Volta are Mossi, a people who are believed to have come into Upper Volta from central or east Africa in the eleventh century. The Mossi were empire builders. By the thirteenth century they were raiding the wealthy trading centers along the Niger River. They established three independent kingdoms before the end of the thirteenth century, Ouagadougou, Yatenga, and Fada-n-Gurma. They also established the Dagomba kingdom in what is now Ghana.

For five centuries, between the fourteenth and nineteenth, the Mossi were in constant wars with the empires of Mali and Songhai. Although they were to suffer any number of defeats, particularly at the hands of Muslim invaders, they resisted conversion to Islam and kept their traditional faiths and customs.

To this date, the Mossi of Upper Volta pay homage to their emperor, the Moro Naba, at his court in Ouagadougou, the capital of Upper Volta; this despite the fact that Upper Volta is today a republic.

The French invaded Upper Volta in 1896, and the country became a French protectorate when the Mossi forces were defeated in Ouagadougou in 1897. In 1919, Upper Volta was declared a French colony.

In 1932, the French divided Upper Volta among its other colonies, Sudan, Niger, and Ivory Coast. But the Mossi insisted on their own identification and, in 1947, Upper Volta was reinstated as a separate and distinct French colony.

In 1960, Upper Volta became an independent republic, with Maurice Yameogo as its first president.

True to the country's volatile nature, however, unrest among the people made Yameogo's presidency a very tentative matter. In 1966, Lieutenant Colonel (now Major General) Aboubakar Sangoule Lamizana, army chief-of-staff, ousted Yameogo from his office and declared himself chief of state.

Lamizana promised a quick return to civilian government, but elections were postponed from year to year, as the army controlled the country.

Finally, in April and May of 1978, the people of Upper Volta went to the polls to elect a new and free government. The results of the election, however, gave no one in the field of four running for the presidency an absolute majority. It took a second round of balloting before Lamizana was returned to his office, as president of the country, with 56 percent of the ballots.

This nomad on his way to a market
is well protected from the sun, wind,
and sand of the Upper Volta desert.

Upper Volta has received considerable assistance from the United States. The United States contributed generously with emergency food assistance during the Upper Volta drought. In 1976, the United States funded an estimated $8 million in development assistance projects. About eighty volunteers of the Peace Corps work in such fields as agriculture, education, and health in Upper Volta.

13
WESTERN SAHARA

Once called Spanish Sahara, Western Sahara is composed of two adjacent zones, Sekia el Hamra and Rio de Oro. Its two most important cities, really towns, are the sea towns, Laayoun (once called El Aioun) in Sekia el Hamra, and Dakhla (once called Villa Cisneros) in Rio de Oro.

The entire territory has a coastline on the South Atlantic Ocean of 490 miles (784 km). Its area is 102,700 square miles (267,020 sq km). It has an estimated population of 160,000. Most of its people are Arabs and Berbers, with some Spaniards and some black Africans. Most are nomads, tending their flocks on the hot and dry, sandy and rocky desert.

With the great nationalist surge that followed the end of World War II, three different peoples laid claim to this territory in the Sahara. Perhaps the discovery of rich phosphate and iron deposits hastened these claims.

In any event, both Morocco and Mauritania declared that they had historic rights to the land. An organization of people living in the land, calling themselves the Popular Front for the Liberation of the Sekia el Hamra and Rio de Oro (known in short as the Polisario), staged a counterclaim.

As early as 1966, the United Nations asked Spain to conduct a referendum in the territory, to determine the will of its inhabitants. The referendum never took place.

On November 6, 1976, King Hassan of Morocco decided to take matters into his own hands. He organized a march of 350,000 unarmed Moroccans into the disputed territory, claiming the land for his country.

Fortunately, there was no violence, and at the urging of the United Nations, King Hassan marched his unarmed invaders back home to Morocco.

Just about a week after the dramatic march of the Moroccans, Spain quietly agreed to give up its colony in Africa. And on February 26, 1976, Spain formally ceded its African holdings to Morocco and Mauritania.

Precisely one day after that dramatic announcement, the Polisario declared its country an independent state and named it the Sahara Arab Democratic Republic.

Equally dramatic was the almost immediate recognition granted the republic by Algeria and several other African nations. The recognition created a rift among the Africans, and did nothing to bring peace to Western Sahara.

On April 4, 1976, Morocco and Mauritania officially divided Western Sahara between them. Mauritania took the southern third of the region, an area the size of South Carolina. Morocco took the northern two-thirds of the territory.

Nomadic women in Western Sahara carry barrels of precious water from a community well to their tents.

This didn't decide the issue either. The Polisario began a guerrilla war. On June 8 and 9, 1976, during a guerrilla raid on Nouakchott, the capital of Mauritania, Sayed-el-Wali, leader of the Saharan independence movement, was killed. This did not halt the guerrilla warfare. The Polisario is still active and the Western Sahara situation is still unresolved.

BIBLIOGRAPHY

Bohannan, P. *Africa and Africans*. New York: Natural History Press, 1964.

Curran, B. D., and Schrock, J. *Area Handbook for Mauritania*. Washington: U.S. Government Printing Office, 1972.

Department of State Publication. *Mali*. Washington: U.S. Government Printing Office, 1979.

Department of State Publication. *Niger*. Washington: U.S. Government Printing Office, 1979.

Department of State Publication. *Upper Volta*. Washington: U.S. Government Printing Office, 1979.

Murphy, J. E. *Understanding Africa*. New York: Crowell, 1978.

Nelson, H. D.; Dobert, M.; McDonald, G. C.; McLaughlin, J.; Marvin, B. J.; and Moeller, P. W. *Area Handbook for Chad*. Washington: U.S. Government Printing Office, 1972.

Page, J. D. *A History of Africa*. New York: Knopf, 1978.

INDEX

Air Mountains, 5
Akjoujt, Mauritania, 47–48
Algeria, 41, 59
Arabic language, 11–12, 33, 36
Arabs, 1–2, 8–9, 19, 49, 52, 57
Atar, Mauritania, 47–48
Atlantic Ocean, 3, 13, 57

Bagoé River, 5
Bakoy River, 5
Bamako, Mali, 44
Bambara people, 8
Baoulé River, 5
Beni Hassan people, 49
Berbers, 1–2, 9, 48–49, 52, 57
Bobo people, 8
Bombara people, 8
Bora Mandaba language, 12
Bornu empire, 52
Boutilimit, Mauritania, 47–48

Chad Liberation Front (Frolinat), 43
Chinguetti, Mauritania, 47–48
Christianity, 20, 33
Congo, 41

Daddah, President Mokta Ould, 49

Dadjo people, 8
Dagomba kingdom, 53
Dakhla, Dio de Oro, 57
Dazaga language, 11
Delim people, 8
Diori, President Hamani, 52
Djado Mountains, 5
Djerma people, 8, 11, 52
Djimet, Colonel Namari, 43

Egyptians, 50
Ethiopia, 40
Europeans, 1, 7, 13, 17, 49. *See also,*
    France; Spain; etc.

Fada-n-Gurma kingdom, 53
Federal Republic of Germany, 13, 17
France, 2, 8, 13, 17, 33, 39, 41, 43, 45,
    49, 52, 55
French Equatorial Africa, 41
French language, 11, 33, 36
Fulani people, 7, 11, 52
Fulbe people, 8

Gabon, 41
Gao, 44
Ghana, 44, 48–49, 52–53

Gorane language, 12
Gourounsi language, 11
Griot caste, 9

Habrei, Prime Minister Hissen, 43
Hassan caste, 9
Hassan, King, 59
Hausa people, 7, 11, 52

Islam, 20–22, 24–25, 32, 34, 53
Ivory Coast, 55
Izarguen people, 8

Kane, Minister Aissata, 49
Kanembou language, 12
Kayes, Mali, 44
Keita, President Modibo, 45
Kountche, Lieutenant Colonel Senyi, 52

Laayoun, Sekia el Hamra, 57
Lake Chad, 3, 6, 13, 15, 40–41
Lamizana, Major General Aboubakar
    Sangoule, 55
Libya, 43
Lobi language, 11
Louly, Lieutenant Colonel Mohamed
    Mahmoud Ould, 49

Maba people, 8
Mali Federation, 45
Malinke people, 8, 44
Malloum, General Felix, 43
Mande people, 8
Mandingo language, 11
Marabouts, 9, 32
Maradi, Niger, 50
Massa language, 12
Massalat people, 8
Maure people, 7–9, 12
Moors, 7
Mopti, Mali, 44

Moro Naba, the, 53
Morocco, 2, 57, 59
Mossi people, 8, 11, 53, 55
Muslims, 1–2, 9, 32, 34, 40–41, 43, 45,
    48–49, 52–53, 57. *See also,* Islam

National Women's Movement, 27
Ndjamena, Chad, 39
Niamey, Niger, 50
Niger River, 5, 53
Nigeria, 3, 41, 43
North Korea, 13, 17
Nouadhibou, Mauritania, 47–48
Nouakchott, Mauritania, 47–48, 60

Ouagadougou, Upper Volta, 53, 55
Oualata, Mauritania, 48
Ouddai language, 12
Oueddei, President Goukouni, 43

Peace Corps, 46, 56
People's Republic of China, 13, 17, 19,
    45
Peruels people, 8
Popular Front for the Liberation of the
    Sekia el Hamra and Rio de Oro (Poli-
    sario), 57, 59–60

Reguibat people, 8
Rio de Oro, 2, 57

Sahara Desert, 2–3, 5–6, 39–41, 47, 50
Saleck, Lieutenant Colonel Moustapha,
    49
Samol language, 11
Sao people, 40
Sara people, 8, 11–12, 28
Sarakole people, 8
Saudi Arabia, 21
Segou, Mali, 44
Sekia el Hamra, 2, 57

Senegal, 45
Senegal River, 5, 47
Shari River, 3
Songhai people, 1, 8–11, 44, 52–53
Soninke people, 8
Soviet Union, 13, 17, 45
Spain, 2, 11, 59
Sudan, 11, 41, 55

Tahoua, Niger, 50
Tama people, 8
Tamashek language, 11
Tamchakett, Mauritania, 48
Tedaga language, 11
Tibesti Mountains, 3
Timbedra, Mauritania, 48
Timbuktu, Mali, 44
Tombalbaye, President Ngarta, 41, 43
Toubou people, 8, 11
Toucoleur people, 8
Touré, Chief Samory, 45
Traoré, President Moussa, 45
Tuareg people, 7–8, 52

Tukulor language, 12

Ubangi-Shari (Central African Republic),
   41
United Nations, 59
United States of America, 13–14, 17, 43,
   46, 56

Wadalan people, 8
Wali, Sayed-el, 60
Wolof people, 8, 12
World War I, 1, 32
World War II, 41, 57

Yameogo, President Maurice, 55
Yatenga kingdom, 53
Yemen, 40
Yugoslavia, 13, 17

Zaghawa kings, 40
Zenaga caste, 9
Zinder, Niger, 50
Zubayr, Rabah, 41